MAGIC TRICKS,
SCIENCE FACTS

FRIEDHOFFER,
THE MADMAN OF MAGIC

magic tricks,
science facts

ILLUSTRATED BY
RICHARD KAUFMAN

PHOTOGRAPHS BY
TIMOTHY WHITE

FRANKLIN WATTS
NEW YORK ◆ LONDON ◆ TORONTO ◆ SYDNEY

Library of Congress Cataloging-in-Publication Data

Friedhoffer, Robert.
Magic tricks, science facts / Friedhoffer, the Madman of Magic ;
illustrated by Richard Kaufman ; photographs by Timothy White.
p. cm.
Includes bibliographical references (p.   ).
Summary: Presents several magic tricks based on principles of
physics, math, chemistry, and physiology.
ISBN 0-531-10902-X
1. Tricks—Juvenile literature. 2. Scientific recreations—
Juvenile literature. [1. Magic tricks. 2. Scientific
recreations.] I. Kaufman, Richard, ill. II. Title.
GV1548.F75 1990
793.8—dc20   89-28487 CIP AC
First Paperback Edition 1990
ISBN 0-531-15186-7
12 11

To my parents,
Nat and Rita Friedhoffer

I hope this would have
made them proud

ACKNOWLEDGMENTS

Thanks to the following folks
for their help and encouragement:

Steve Mark, Suzanne Phillips,
Iris Rosoff, Margie Leather,
Raphael Bogarin, Imam and Evelyn,
Timothy White, Richard Kaufman,
Brian Werther, Steve Pinsky,
Bob Wolen, Lorraine Zeller,
Lee Freed, Lou Stevens,
Abbi Lindner, Dr. Helene Mayer,
David Pedowitz, Carl Stenquist,
Tom Ladshaw, George Magdaleno,
Art Kahn, Harvey and Rona Maltz,
Annette Choynacki, Trish Sands,
and Eric and Sara Rosoff

CONTENTS

"Any sufficiently advanced technology
is indistinguishable from magic."

Arthur C. Clarke
The Lost Worlds of 2001

"The magic of the past is
the science of the future."

Bob Friedhoffer

MAGIC TRICKS, SCIENCE FACTS

A NOTE TO PARENTS AND TEACHERS

This book attempts to help children become interested in the study of the sciences while teaching them rudimentary principles. It does this by stripping away some of the mysteries associated with science and technology.

Scientific and mathematical principles presented as magic or puzzles have an allure that appeals to many children, even those with marginal scientific interests. This book was written to show children that science and math can be fun and exciting, as well as useful. It will:

- make the pursuit of science a game that children will want to play
- be a useful tool to children, allowing them to learn to express themselves in public through the performance of magic tricks
- help them to develop a knowledge of the psychology of working with people
- by the very nature of the performance, help them to learn to think on their feet

PREFACE

When I was a kid, I was very nosy. I always wanted to know how and why things worked. What were their secrets? I'd constantly take things apart to find out what made them tick. Occasionally that would get me into all sorts of trouble, because I couldn't put them back together again.

One day I discovered magic and learned that it too had secrets. I wanted to know about those secrets. I studied books, talked to amateur magicians, and bought tricks. I was in heaven.

In school we were taught the secrets of physics, chemistry, and biology. To master these secrets, I studied books, talked to my teachers, and experimented in the labs. Heaven again!

Today I enjoy combining my two interests. I perform magic on stage and whenever possible include science-based tricks in my act. The secrets of magic and science are very old, and the number of new tricks that can be invented using these principles is practically limitless.

I hope that you enjoy learning these scientific magic tricks, and their secrets, as much as I've enjoyed putting them together for you.

Bob Friedhoffer aka
The Madman of Magic

INTRODUCTION

The performance of magic works because of "secrets." Magic is traditionally shrouded in mystery. If there were no secrets, magic would consist of *someone* standing on stage doing a bunch of "dumb things" that everyone knows. There would be no mysteries.

Keeping the secrets of magic to yourself is important if you wish to fool your audience. If the spectators are kept in the dark, they'll be impressed. If you tell them the secrets behind the tricks, *you* will be that someone standing on stage doing a bunch of "dumb things."

This book was written as a *magic book*. Please help keep the secrets.

◆ ◆ ◆

Before you perform any magic tricks successfully, you have to make a few decisions. You have to decide:

- that you want to do the trick
- that you're willing to spend some time learning the trick
- that you're ready to practice the trick until you can perform it well

Practicing the trick is the hardest part, but it is also the most rewarding. Diligent practice will allow you to fool your audience and keep you from worrying, "What do I do next?" while performing the trick.

◆ ◆ ◆

"As soon as the technical side of the trick is mentioned, the student must turn to the dramatic, which is the most important as far as the effect is concerned." H. J. Burlingame, 1897

◆ ◆ ◆

To perform any of the tricks in this book, you should know if the trick you're about to do is based on science or math. If it's based on science, you must know which area of science—physics, chemistry, or physiology.

You must also consider the venue, or the area or place where the performance is to take place. It can be either on stage or close to the spectators.

The tricks in this book are divided into four groups: physics, math, chemistry, and physiology. Each trick is broken into sections that give information on the effect produced by the trick, the props used, and the routine and method of performing the trick. There is also a follow-up note that further explains the science behind the magic.

These sections are described below.

EFFECT

When we watch a movie or TV show, we get so involved with the action that we forget that we are watching actors. We forget that we are just watching a story. For a while we actually believe that what's happening is real. That's what should happen to your audience, whether it's one person or fifty, when you perform a trick.

The effect is not what actually happens. It's what the audience *thinks* happens.

ROUTINE

This is the plot of the trick. When performing, you must tell some sort of story, even if it's done silently through pantomime. If the story is interesting, the audience will pay attention and enjoy your performance.

Most of the tricks in this book include a routine. This makes the mastering of the trick easier for you. A few of the tricks are given without involved routines. They are included so that you can develop a routine of your own.

PROPS

These are the items that you need for the performance. You must prepare the props, learn where they go in your performing area, and get used to handling them in a natural manner. If you don't prepare your props, the trick won't work properly.

Always handle your props with care. If they break, you won't be able to use them again.

Be careful when handling any chemicals. All of the chemicals recommended in this book can be handled safely, but must be treated with respect. Some of them can be dangerous if used in an improper or sloppy way.

METHOD

This is a combination of *effect, routine,* and *props.* When these are put together following the instructions in *method,* you end up with a magical performance.

NOTE

This section gives you a greater understanding of why or how the trick works. Included are some of the "real secrets" of science magic.

physics

HAUNTED MATCHBOX

EFFECT

A matchbox moves under its own power.

ROUTINE

"You've all seen the movie *Ghostbusters,* right? Well, I'm going to show you what could happen if ghosts really existed and could haunt everyday objects."

After saying these opening lines, take a small box of wooden matches from your pants pocket and place it on your upturned right palm, pointing to the fingertips.

"Watch carefully, because what you're about to see enters the realm of the impossible."

Imitate a drill sergeant. "To the right, march!" The box uncannily moves to the right. "To the left, march!" It moves to the left. "Forward, march!" It moves forward, right toward your fingertips.

"Open up!" is the next command. Slowly, in a real spooky way, the box opens on its own.

With that, you hand the matchbox to a spectator to examine. The person will find no clue as to how this trick works. The matchbox is not connected to anything. It was apparently just resting on your open palm. There must be ghosts!

PROPS

a small matchbox filled with matches
a 2-foot (.61-m) length of thin nylon monofilament
    fishing line or sewing thread
a safety pin

(The preparation should be quite clear by reading the following description and referring to the illustrations.)
    The sleeve of the box is prepared by making a small slit ⅛ inch (.32 cm) long at the center of each end. The nylon thread is tied at one end to the safety pin, with a simple knot at the other end. The knotted end is then placed into the slit of the sleeve. The matchbox is placed into the sleeve so that the thread is pushed into the box.

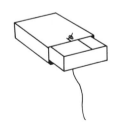

METHOD

Attach the safety pin to a belt loop on the right side of your pants. You will have to experiment with the thread or fishing line to find the proper length. Then place the box in your right pants pocket. Now you are ready to begin.

Remove the box from your pocket with your right hand. With your left hand, place the box on your right palm. The threaded end of the box should be facing your wrist, with the thread underneath the box. Run the thread between your middle and ring fingers so that it is hidden from view by the box.

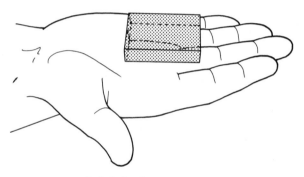

Initial placement

By moving your hand slightly forward, the thread tightens up. It will appear to the audience as though the matchbox is moving across your hand. If you practice moving slowly, the movement of the hand will not be seen.

Turning the box to the right and to the left is accomplished by placing the box either to the right or to the left side of the center of your palm. Placed to the right, it will go right; placed to the left, it will go left.

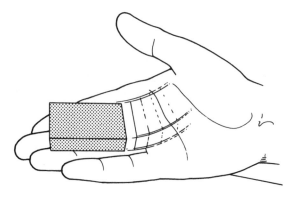

Forward march!

To open the box, twist it 180° (one half-turn) so that the thread end faces your fingertips, thread still on the bottom, the edge of the box just at the point where the fingers meet the palm of the hand. Slowly moving your hand forward will cause the box to slide open.

When the box is fully open, hand the drawer to a spectator with your left hand. Then pick up the sleeve with the left hand, pulling it away from the thread. Hand that to a spectator; the thread will fall unnoticed to your side.

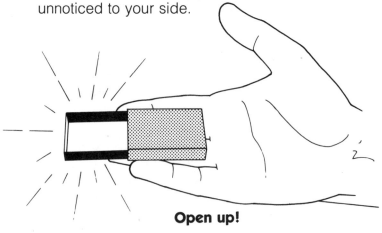

Open up!

NOTE

To change the direction of a force, you can use a wheel and a rope. The wheel is called a pulley. The rope runs around the wheel.

For example, if you wanted to lift a heavy load to the top of a building, you could attach a pulley at the roof, with a rope running through it. The rope would have to be twice as long as the distance from the rooftop to the ground. You would attach a load, like a piece of wood, to one end of the rope and pull on the other end. The wood would be transported to the rooftop. You would pull down and the wood would rise.

That's what is meant by changing the direction of the force. Using a simple pulley system like the above, the load moves the same distance as the force moves.

In this trick, the thread takes the place of the rope, and the edge of the box that the thread rubs against takes the place of the wheel.

RISING RING

EFFECT

A borrowed finger ring breaks the bonds of gravity.

ROUTINE

Start by saying, "Scientists have claimed that anti-gravity is impossible, but there have been recent experiments with superconductors that have people wondering. I've been studying this phenomenon of anti-gravity and I'd like to perform a little demonstration of it for you."

Borrow a ring from a spectator. Place the ring on a pencil that's taken from your pocket. Hold the pencil by its point in one hand, the eraser in the other, directly in front of your body.

"If you watch closely, you will see that the ring first stays suspended around the pencil, then slowly rises."

Turn the pencil so that the eraser end is pointed upward, then let go of the eraser. To the audi-

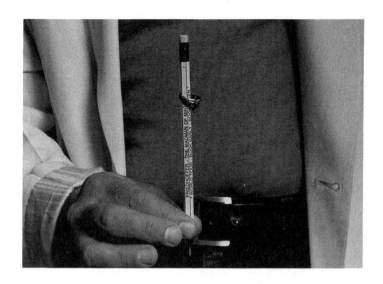

Breaking the bonds of gravity

ence's surprise, the ring does just as you said it would.

When the ring rises to the top of the pencil, take it off and return the ring to its owner, along with the pencil.

PROPS

a wooden pencil with an eraser at one end
a piece of black thread

The eraser has a slit across the top, about ⅛ inch (.32 cm) deep. The thread has a knot on one end. The knot is secured within the slit and the other end of the thread is tied to a button on a jacket or shirt. You'll need to experiment to determine the appropriate length of thread.

METHOD

Because of the thread, this trick is best done on stage. You should wear dark clothing to camouflage the thread.

When you take the pencil from your pocket, have the thread run from the eraser to the point of the pencil. Place the ring on the pencil so it goes over the thread.

When you hold the pencil by the point, eraser end up, the thread will support the ring and keep it from falling to the floor.

If you move the hand holding the pencil away from your body, it will appear that the ring rises. (See illustration.)

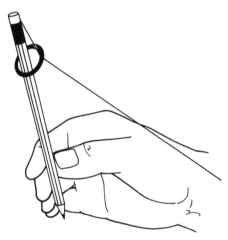

NOTE

In this trick, thread acts as a rope, as in the *Haunted Matchbox* (see page 25). The edge of the ring acts as a simple pulley, changing the direction of the force applied from a motion parallel to the floor to an upward direction.

MYSTIC TUBES
OF CAIRO

EFFECT

Egyptian tubes move in a mysterious way.

ROUTINE

"Many years ago, when the Egyptian pyramids were being searched, strange items were unearthed. I'm going to show you two of the oddest items that were found in a small pyramid discovered in Cairo, Egypt. I don't have the actual pieces here, of course, since they are kept in the British Museum. What I do have are authentic reproductions."

At this point, bring out two separate, intricately decorated cardboard tubes, each with a string running through it.

Pick up one of the tubes (tube 1) by the ends of the string in each hand, hands outstretched to the full length of the string. Turn your hands so that they are perpendicular to the floor, that is, one hand above the other. The tube will be kept from falling off the string by your bottom hand.

A mystic tube of Cairo

"This first tube has the ability to suspend the law of gravity for a few moments at the command of the person in control—me!"

With this statement, change the positions of your hands so that the tube is now on top. As it starts to slide down the string, say, "Stop!" The tube stops. Say, "Go!" and the tube begins to fall again.

You are in complete control.

Put down the first tube and pick up the second (tube 2). "Now I will show you something even stranger. The first tube can suspend gravity; this tube can reverse gravity. None of the scientists who've examined this have figured out the secret; they just know that it works."

Hold the ends of the string the same way you did the first tube. This tube starts off suspended in the middle of the string. Give the command, "Fall!" and the tube slowly starts to descend. Say, "Stop!" and it stops. Now say, "Rise!" and it slowly climbs up the string.

When your demonstration is over, put the tubes away, far from the prying eyes and hands of your audience.

PROPS

To make the tubes, you need:

2 cardboard tubes, like those found in rolls of paper towels
3 pieces of string, each about 3 feet (1 m) long
a thin plastic curtain ring, about ¼ inch (.64 cm) to ½ inch (1.28 cm) in diameter
cellophane tape
construction paper

Tube 1

Cut a piece of construction paper so that its dimensions are ½ inch (1.28 cm) by 8 inches (2.44 cm). One-half inch (1.28 cm) from each end, cut or punch a small hole, about ⅛ inch (.32 cm) in diameter.

X-ray view of Tube 1

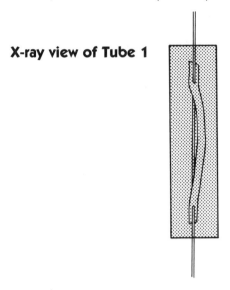

Run one of the strings through each hole so that the construction paper is in the center of the string. Place the paper along with the string in the center of one of the tubes.

Keeping the construction paper as flat as possible, carefully tape it to the inside of the tube. Make sure that the string runs freely through the tube without being taped. Decorate the outside of the tube to suggest Egyptian hieroglyphics.

Tube 2

Thread a string through the second tube. Secure one end of the string to the inside of the tube with tape. Do this near one end of the tube.

X-ray view of Tube 2

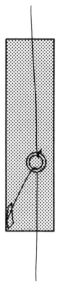

Tie the third string by an end to the curtain ring. Thread the curtain ring onto the tube's string, and push the tube's string back into the tube, so that it comes out of the other end, where it is taped. Slowly pull the end now emerging from the tube so that the curtain ring is inside the tube.

Decorate the tube in an Egyptian motif.

METHOD

Tube 1 works by friction. If the string is held rather loosely, the tube will fall to the lowest point because of gravity. If the string is held tightly, friction created by the string against the edges of the holes in the construction paper is a force greater than gravity. Therefore, the tube will not fall.

Tube 2 works like a pulley. The curtain ring takes the place of the wheel; the thread, the place of rope. By having the string tied to the curtain ring on the bottom of the tube, all you have to do is pull up on the top string and the tube will rise.

Once again, you have used a simple pulley to change direction.

NOTE ON
MECHANICAL MOVEMENT

The three tricks demonstrating the simple pulley—*Haunted Matchbox, Rising Ring,* and *Mystic Tubes of Cairo*—have all been included to show that the same mechanism can be used in a variety of ways. Think about these principles of movement, then come up with interesting variations of your own.

THE STRENGTH
OF FOUR

EFFECT

Show your power to be greater than that of four
people.

ROUTINE

"I'd like to show you a stunt that a strong man in the
circus would have done many years ago."

With that opening line, ask four people in the
audience to come up to assist you. All of them
should weigh about the same.

Have them stand facing each other, in pairs,
about two feet apart.

Give each pair a broomstick to hold out in front
of them, each person holding one end.

"Now I'm going to take a rope and wind it
around the sticks a few times. When I finish, I'm
going to hold on to one end of the rope and pull."

Say to your four helpers: "Your job is to pull
steadily on the broomsticks and not let me pull them

together. Don't forget; there are four of you pulling against one of me."

At this point you start to pull on the rope. No matter how hard your helpers strain, you manage to pull the two broomsticks together.

PROPS

2 sturdy broomsticks
a clothesline, about 50 feet (15 m) long

METHOD

Tie one end of the rope to a broomstick. Keeping the sticks about 2 feet (.60 m) apart, loop the rope around them five times, in zigzag fashion.

the rope looped around the broomsticks

When this is done, pull steadily on the free end of the rope. Assuming that you're about the same weight and strength as each of your helpers, you will be able to pull the sticks together. (See illustration.)

EXPLANATION

In this trick, you have created a pulley system called a block and tackle. Instead of having the pulley change the direction of force, you are using it to multiply your exerted force. A block and tackle multiplies force by the number of wheels; in this case, the number of turns of rope around the broomsticks (five times on each stick, or ten times). This primitive block and tackle you have created will increase your power by about ten times, depending on the exact number of turns the rope has taken. That's where I got the name for the trick.

The block-and-tackle principle can be found in use every day. You might see it in operation at an auto shop, where it is used to haul an engine from a car, or at a construction site, where a crane is used to lift a heavy pallet of bricks.

OLD SALTS' CARD TRICK

EFFECT

Find a selected card with the aid of a saltshaker.

ROUTINE

Tell the following story:

"My uncle was a sailor—an old salt. He was one of the greatest guys you could ever meet. He knew how to tie fifty different knots, told marvelous stories, and did card tricks that would leave you amazed. He did one with a saltshaker that's unbelievable. Let me show it to you."

Take out a deck of cards. "First, you have to shuffle the deck."

Have a spectator shuffle the cards.

"Now place the cards on the table and cut the deck in half."

After the spectator has done that, say, "Take a look at the top card of either pile, show it around, and place it back on top of the pile."

Gesture at the pile with the card that the spectator just looked at and say, "Now place the other pile on top, right here," touching the back of the selected card.

The card has been selected and lost in the middle of the deck. Take a full saltshaker out of your pocket and say, "My uncle was an old salt, and since this was his trick, we'll use some 'old salt.' Just sprinkle a little bit on top of the deck." When the participant has done this, retrieve the saltshaker. Gently tap the side of the deck with the shaker. The deck will separate at one particular point. Have the spectator turn over the first face-down card at the separation. It will be the selected card.

The old salt's card trick

PROPS

a deck of cards
a full saltshaker

METHOD

The strange part of this trick is that salt really is used to find the card, but not in the way that the spectator thinks. While the spectator looks at the selected card, put a little bit of salt on the end of your right index finger. As you gesture at the pile with the selected card on top, let your finger brush against the top card (the selected one), leaving some salt on it. Don't leave too much or it will be noticed. When the person replaces the rest of the deck on top of that card, salt the entire pack.

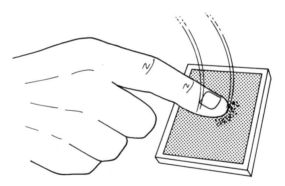

leave some salt on the selected card

Tapping the side of the deck with the salt-shaker causes the cards to separate, right at the card where you secretly placed the salt. The reason that you have the spectator salt the top of the deck is so that if any salt is seen on top of the selected card, there's an excuse for it.

NOTE

The reason that this trick works is the same reason why your bike will skid on a loose surface, like gravel or sand—reduced friction. Friction has been lowered at the point where the selected card lies through the addition of the salt. The grains of salt act as ball bearings, making the selected card slide more easily than any of the other cards.

CAN YOU
CATCH IT?

EFFECT

A deck of cards is tossed through the air and stays together.

ROUTINE

As the prelude to the trick, remove a deck of cards from its case.

Ask one of the audience members to stand up and get ready to catch the deck, because you're going to throw it to her. Then toss the deck.

You'll be left holding the two jokers, and you will say, "We don't need these for the trick."

The deck will fly through the air without separating and your helper will catch it.

If caught properly, the deck won't scatter but will stay together, as if by magic.

PROPS

a deck of cards complete with two jokers and a
    card case

METHOD

Take the cards from the case, placing the case out of the way.

Hold the deck in the palm of your throwing hand, as shown in the illustration. The back of the hand is to the floor. The deck should be squared into a block, the top and bottom cards of the block the jokers jogged back about 1 inch (2.5 cm) into the base of the thumb; the thumb on top, the other fingers on the bottom.

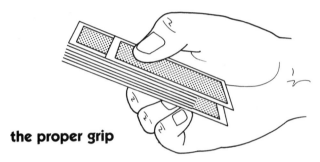

the proper grip

With a light, flat, underhand tossing motion, lightly release the pressure of the thumb and fingers, letting the deck slide from between the top and bottom cards.

Two things happen at this point:

- The top and bottom cards (the jokers) are held in place by the thumb and fingers, which automatically close, holding those two cards.
- The deck travels through the air in a flat arc, maintaining its integrity as a complete block.

With some practice, the author has successfully thrown a deck a distance of 25 feet (7.62 m).

NOTE

Gravity is acting upon all of the cards with the same force. Therefore, none will fall faster than any other.

If the cards are new and flat and are pressed together just before the toss, air pressure will tend to make them stick together in a block. A minor vacuum is created between each card.

The reason that you hold the two cards back is to reduce the chance of a card or cards sticking to your fingers accidentally when you release the deck. There will be less friction created by the deck sliding between the two cards than by the deck sliding between your fingers.

THE GREAT ESCAPE

EFFECT

A selected card is discovered in a unique way.

ROUTINE

After the deck is tossed to your helper in *Can You Catch It?* (see page 46), have her shuffle the cards.

Tell her to take a card from the deck, hand the deck back to you, and remember the card still in her possession, which you tell her is the famous secret agent card. (Have her show it to some other people in case she forgets it.) Then have her place the card in the center of the deck, or, as we shall call it, the SASA (Society Against Secret Agents) airliner.

Cut the deck twice, so that no one knows where the secret agent is located, and place the jokers (now to be known as the SASA thug cards) on the top and bottom of the deck, telling the audience that they have been sent by SASA Central to kidnap the secret agent.

The secret agent escapes

Have your helper stand back, and once again toss the deck to her (as in *Can You Catch It?*), only this time one card leaps from the deck during its flight and slowly drifts to the floor. Upon picking up the card and examining it, the audience sees that the card is the secret agent card. Tell them that the secret agent has successfully escaped the clutches of SASA, parachuting to safety.

PROPS

a deck of cards, complete with jokers

METHOD

The first step is to find the secret agent card. An easy way to do this is by using a "corner short," or key card.

To make this, take a card, not a joker, from the deck and place it facedown in front of you. Using a nail clipper, slightly round off the upper left-hand and lower right-hand corners of the card. When this key card is in the squared-up deck, it's easy to find. Hold the facedown deck in a dealing position and riffle the upper left-hand corners of the cards with your left thumb, top to bottom. With a little practice, you will find that there is a clicking sound and that the riffling tends to stop when you get to the key card. After a bit of practice, you'll get the knack of finding the key card.

Now that you have the key card, here's how you use it to find the selected card.

After your helper has shuffled the deck, selected a card, and returned the deck to you, find the key card, as explained above. When you find the key, cut it to the bottom of the deck. If you can't find the key card right away, cut the deck and riffle again, until you locate it.

Once the key is on the bottom, have your helper place the selected (secret agent) card facedown on top of the deck. Then cut the deck in half, so that the secret agent card is in the center of the pack, with the key card resting on top.

Cut the deck once again at the key card, making sure it goes on the bottom, leaving the selected card on top of the deck. Meanwhile, explain to the audience that you are mixing up the deck so that no one can find the secret agent card.

the proper grip

If you can't find the key after riffling and cutting four or five times, realize that your helper may have selected it. This is okay, since all you have to do is have the card placed in the center of the deck, then riffle down and cut it to the top of the deck.

Now that you have the selected card on top of the deck, you want it to separate from the pack and float to the floor when you toss the deck to your helper. To do this part of the trick, keep the deck squared up as in *Can You Catch It?*, but slide the selected card back, so that an inch or so of it projects off the rear of the deck. Then take the SASA thug cards (jokers) and place them on the top and bottom of the deck, extending an inch or so past the secret agent card.

All that's left to do is to toss the deck to your helper again.

The difference between this version and *Can You Catch It?* is that the selected card will fall to the floor as the deck lands intact in your helper's hands.

NOTE

If all of the cards were squared up with the rest of the deck, then thrown and caught well, they would stay in a block as in *Can You Catch It?*

The reason that the selected card flies out of the deck by "itself" is that air resistance acts on the extended portion of the card and forces it from the top of the deck. The extended card acts as a sail. Bodies that travel through air are slowed down (retarded) by air resistance. The amount of resistance is increased when a) the cross-section area is increased, b) when the speed of the moving object is increased, or c) when the object becomes less streamlined.

HYDROSTATIC GLASS

EFFECT

Water remains suspended in a glass that's turned upside down.

ROUTINE

Fill a glass to its rim with water. Cover the mouth of the glass with an index card.

Holding the card in place, turn the glass upside down and "command" the water to remain in place. Remove your hand from the card. Miraculously, the water and card stay put. After a few moments, command the water and card to fall (make sure that you're standing over a bucket or sink to catch the water). The water and card obey.

PROPS

a plastic drinking glass
an index card larger than the mouth of the glass
a bucket of water

The water stays suspended

METHOD

Drill a small hole (about 1/16 inch; .16 cm) into the side of the glass, near the bottom. (See illustration.)

glass preparation

covering the small hole

Pick up the glass with your right hand, covering the hole with your right thumb. Block the hole so that when the glass is filled, the water won't run out. Fill the glass by dipping it into the bucket.

Now, using your left hand, cover the mouth of the glass with the index card. Place your hand lightly on top of the index card, keeping the card in place.

Slowly turn the glass, with the card over its mouth, upside down, making sure that your right thumb still covers the hole at the bottom of the glass. Remove your left hand from the card. If all has been done correctly, the water remains in the glass, covered by the card.

When you wish to end the trick, "command" the water to fall by moving your thumb slightly away from the hole. Make sure that the glass is over the bucket when you do this part of the trick.

NOTE

The water stays inside of the glass because the air pressure pushing up on the card is a greater force than the gravity pulling down on it.

Air pressure keeps the card and water in place. When your thumb moves away from the hole, air moves into the glass. The air pressure on the inside of the glass now equals that on the outside.

Gravity is now the stronger force, and the index card and water fall.

THE EVER-POPULAR FLOATING BALLOON

EFFECT

A balloon floats, totally under your control.

ROUTINE

Standing in front of a small table, face the audience and say:

"Many people in many countries have spent millions of dollars trying to develop anti-gravity machines. The first person to perfect one will be rich beyond her or his wildest dreams. Airplanes won't be necessary anymore. Neither will cars, boats, or trucks. Special terminals like train stations or airports won't be used. The ideal anti-gravity machine could take off and land just about anyplace.

"I'm about to show you a trick that demonstrates what anti-gravity would be like."

On the table is a box. Reach into the box and take out a round balloon, which you blow up and tie off.

"I'm about to show you a trick that demonstrates
what anti-gravity would be like."

Start some tape-recorded music to put people in the mood for what's to follow.

Hold the balloon over the box, say the magic words, and let go of the balloon. It floats, moving at your command, totally unsupported.

Pass a hoop over and around the balloon, proving that nothing is supporting it.

PROPS

an oscillating fan
a cassette tape player and music
a cardboard box, large enough to conceal the fan
    and tape player
a 10-inch (.039-cm) round balloon
a 14-inch (.028-cm) hoop

METHOD

The fan, the secret behind this great illusion, should be concealed within the box on the table, along with the cassette tape player.

Aim the fan upward, out of the box. The music is played to cover the noise of the fan.

Reach into the box, start the music, then the fan.

Inflate the balloon, tie it off, then place it directly in the center of the fan's current of air. Release the balloon.

If placed properly, the balloon will stay suspended in the center of the airflow, even though the fan is moving back and forth, until you shut off the fan or until the balloon is removed.

Moving your hands in front of the balloon, making magical gestures, will make it seem as if the balloon is following your commands. Passing the large hoop around the balloon will add to the effect.

To end the performance, remove the balloon, toss it to the audience, shut off the fan, and then stop the music.

NOTE

The balloon is supported by the air current, which is exerting enough force to overcome the force of gravity.

The balloon stays within the updraft created by the fan because of *Bernoulli's principle*. This principle states that the fast-moving current of air exerts less sidewards pressure than a slow-moving current. If the balloon starts to drift away from the fan's air current, the higher pressure from the slower-moving surrounding air pushes it back to the center of the airflow.

COLD CONTROL

EFFECT

You can apparently control temperature with magic.

ROUTINE

While sitting at your kitchen table, sip from a glass of water filled with ice cubes. A water-filled pitcher is on the table next to you.

Remark to your friends that ice melts above 32°F (Fahrenheit), or 0°C (Celsius), and will stay solid below that temperature.

Measure the temperature of the water in your glass with a thermometer.

Remove the thermometer from the glass and drink all of the water, getting rid of the ice cubes at the same time.

Bring up the fact that you have been studying magic and have found the secret to controlling temperature, if only to a few degrees.

Fill the glass with water and ice cubes from the pitcher. Place the thermometer in the glass and make mystical passes over it. In a few moments, the temperature of the water falls below 32° F.

PROPS

a glass of water filled with ice cubes
a pitcher of cold salt water
saltwater ice cubes made with table salt
a Fahrenheit thermometer that measures between
    0° and 90°

METHOD

After finishing the first glass of water, refill the glass with salt water and saltwater cubes from the pitcher.

NOTE

When Gabriel Fahrenheit was experimenting with temperatures at sea level, he discovered that water always froze at a certain temperature (32°) and always boiled at a certain temperature (212°). (The Celsius scale records the freezing temperature of water as 0° and the boiling temperature as 100°.) He also discovered that if you added chemicals to water, the freezing temperature could be altered.

Adding salt lowers the freezing point of water. This fact is used every winter in areas of the world where it snows. Salt is spread on icy, snowy sidewalks and roadways to hasten melting.

LAW-BREAKING PAPER CLIPS

EFFECT

Ordinary paper clips make a mockery of "the laws of gravity."

ROUTINE

Display five copper paper clips, hooked together into a chain. Ask your friends to disconnect them.

When they've finished, pick up a paper clip between your index finger and thumb, holding it an inch or two above the surface of the table.

Take a second paper clip and touch it to the first. They stick together without being linked and start to form a chain, actually defying the laws of gravity. It's just like magic.

Do the same with the remaining clips. They all cling together in a chain.

Once your friends have had a chance to see this minor miracle, command the clips to separate and drop to the table, which they do.

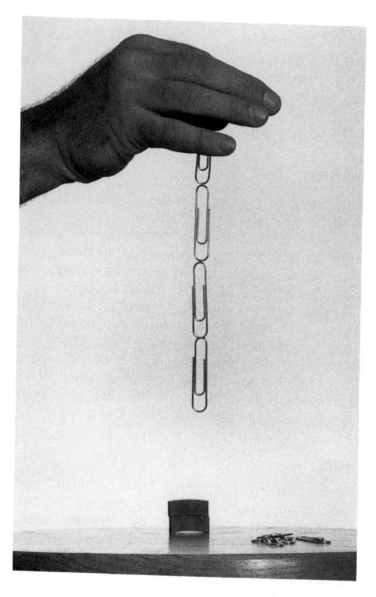

The paper clip trick. The magnet is exposed for photo purposes.

PROPS

wood or plastic-topped table
strong magnet
strong duct tape
copper-clad, steel paper clips (available in office
    supply stores)

METHOD

Conceal the magnet under the tabletop. Secure it with the duct tape.

After the chain is disconnected by your friends, pick up the first paper clip and hold it directly over the magnet. If the magnet is strong enough, the magnetic field will penetrate the tabletop.

When the second clip is touched to the first, the magnetic field will travel through one clip to the other, making them stick together. This happens with each succeeding paper clip. To end the trick, move your hand away from the magnet, simultaneously commanding the clips to fall. The clips apparently separate at your command.

NOTE

Steel is affected by magnetic fields because it's an alloy (mixture) of iron, which has magnetic properties. Copper is not affected by magnetic fields. Anyone who knows about magnetism will see the copper-colored clips and assume that they are nonmagnetic.

The magnetic field transfers into the steel of the paper clip. The paper clip is turned into a magnet for the length of time that it's in the field. This is called magnetic induction, or induced magnetism.

CHOP CHOP'S CUP

EFFECT

A small aluminum foil ball appears and vanishes from a paper cup.

PROPS

a small bar or button magnet, ½ inch by 1 inch (1.3 cm by 2.6 cm)

a paper cup with a slightly recessed bottom

a piece of aluminum foil large enough to wrap around the cup

glue and tape

Glue the magnet to the outside bottom of the cup. When the glue is dry, wrap the cup with a single layer of foil, covering the magnet and the entire outside of the cup. Tape it all in place.

a small piece of steel wool rolled into a ball about ½ inch to ¾ inch (1.3 cm to 1.9 cm) in diameter

a piece of aluminum foil large enough to wrap
around the steel wool ball, totally covering it,
making it look like a foil ball
Note: If the cup and ball are made properly,
you can place the ball inside the cup, turn the cup
upside down, and the steel wool ball will remain
suspended.

a piece of aluminum foil large enough so that when
it's crumpled into a ball, it will be the same size
as the foil-covered steel wool ball
a table covered with a soft surface, such as a terry
cloth towel or a magician's close-up pad
(available from magic supply stores)

METHOD

No one should be aware that there are two balls
being used. Before you show this trick to your
friends, put the magnetic aluminum foil/steel wool
ball inside the cup.

Place the foil-covered cup on the table, mouth
down, with the magnetic ball inside, clinging to the
bottom of the cup. The ball stays in place because
of the attraction between the magnet and the steel
wool. Your audience should not suspect that there
is anything inside the cup.

Display the extra piece of foil. Crumple it into
a ball, about the same size as the one in the cup,
and place it on the table. It should look like the
magnetic ball.

Pick up the cup, mouth down, and place it
gently over the foil ball.

Ask your friends if they know where the ball is.
They should say that it is under the cup.

Tell them they're correct.

Gently pick up the cup, still mouth down, revealing the foil ball. Place it to the right of the cup. When putting the cup down this time, do it hard enough to dislodge the hidden magnetic ball, but not hard enough to crush the cup.

The soft surface should muffle the sound of the falling ball.

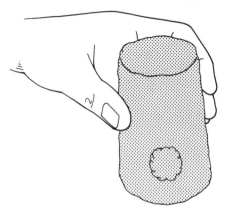

Ignore the cup for now.

Pick up the visible ball and place it in your right pants pocket.

Ask your friends, "Where is the ball now?"

They will say, "In your pocket."

Tell them, "You aren't paying attention!"

Pick up the cup and reveal the magnetic ball.

Pick up the ball in one hand, the cup in the other, and drop the ball into the cup.

Turn the mouth of the cup into your right palm and make believe that you are pouring the ball into your hand.

Close your hand as if you're holding the ball. At this point, the ball is still in the cup, held magnetically to the bottom. The cup should be placed mouth down on the table. Do not dislodge the magnetic ball.

Ask where the ball is. Your friends should say, "In your hand."

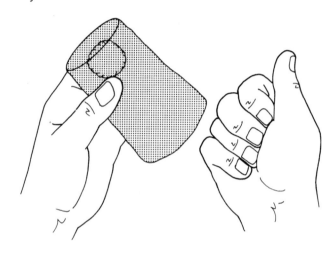

Show them that they are once again wrong by opening your hand. Reach into your right pocket and pull out the foil ball.

Pick up the cup and turn it mouth up. Don't let the audience look into it. Drop the visible ball into the cup, on top of the magnetic ball, then place it away from your friends' prying eyes and hands.

This is a basic routine for a great prop.

If you wish, professional models may be bought at magic supply stores, along with instructions for extended routines.

NOTE

This trick makes use of the fact that a magnetic field may penetrate nonmagnetic materials, that is, the paper cup and aluminum foil. This fact is used in many ways, such as in magnetic seals on refrigerator doors or magnetic sensing units on burglar alarms.

This effect is named after its inventor, magician Al Wheatley, whose stage name was Chop Chop.

math

CAN YOU COUNT?

EFFECT

Prove to your friends that they can't count.

ROUTINE

Tell your friends that you will count and that you want them to help. You will say the first number in a sequence, they will say the second, you will say the next, and so on.

In a short while, they will make a mistake that is so simple, yet shows that doing things by rote, by a fixed routine, can lead to false conclusions.

PROPS

None

METHOD

Say to your friends: "I bet that you can't count. Let's try an experiment. I'm going to start counting. I'll give you the first number, then you give me the next number in sequence, then it's my turn, then yours, then mine. We'll go on like that until one of us makes a mistake."

When they agree, say, "What number comes after four thousand ninety-three?"

They will say, "Four thousand ninety-four."

You say, "Four thousand ninety-five."

They say, "Four thousand ninety-six."

You, "Four thousand ninety-seven."

They, "Four thousand ninety-eight."

You, "Four thousand ninety-nine."

They will probably then say, "Five thousand."

And you say, "You're wrong. The correct answer is four thousand one hundred."

NOTE

This trick/gag shows how you can influence people's thinking by the way you say something.

The victims are lulled into thinking one way because they are reciting the numbers by rote. They stop analyzing what you're saying and fall into the trap that you've laid for them.

FOURTH-DIMENSIONAL SCULPTURE

EFFECT

Create an impossible paper sculpture.

ROUTINE

You're seated across a table from your audience. On the table are a number of plain index cards, a pair of scissors, a glue stick, and a folded piece of decorated cardboard that can be used as a screen.

Pick up one of the index cards and proceed to cut three slits in it. As you're doing this, tell your audience:

"My study of magic, combined with my knowledge of science, has enabled me to place objects into the fourth dimension and then to retrieve them. I can do this by making an object vanish, then having it reappear. But that isn't proof that it's entered another dimension. What I'm about to do will wipe any doubts from your mind and leave you with concrete evidence that I've been successful."

The impossible sculpture

Place the scissors and the index card on the table. Open the screen so that a small work area will be shielded from the eyes of your spectators.

Place the glue stick, the slit index card, and an uncut card out of view behind the screen.

Reach behind the screen and, in a matter of moments, bring out the strange sculpture.

"You will notice," you say, "that no matter how we bend the centerpiece, it looks wrong. The sculpture has been constructed in a way that is totally impossible in our world. The only possible solution is that I have entered the fourth dimension."

With that, hand the sculpture to a spectator, letting him keep it as a souvenir, and proceed to some other mind-boggling feat of scientific magic.

PROPS

unlined index cards

scissors

a glue stick

a piece of cardboard, folded in half to act
     as a screen and labeled "Fourth-Dimensional
     Transporter"

METHOD

Cut three slits in one of the cards, as in *Routine.*
Put the props behind the cardboard screen.

    Pick up the slit index card with both hands,
keeping it parallel to the table, the slit side toward
the audience.

    Your right thumb should be on top of the card,
with your right-hand fingers directly underneath; the
left-hand fingers should be on top with the left thumb
underneath.

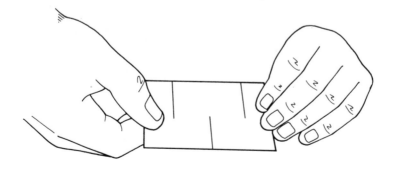

Hold the right hand steady and twist the left-hand fingers so that the left thumb is now on top (see illustration). If done properly, half of the card should rotate in a forward direction.

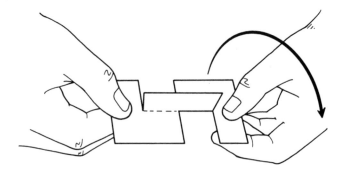

Place the card on the table and crease the middle section in both directions.

You have now made the basic fourth-dimensional sculpture. Using the glue stick, glue the bottom of the sculpture to an uncut index card. When this is done, remove the screen and display the sculpture to your audience.

After the glue has dried, hand the sculpture to the spectators.

If you wish, before you begin folding, have one of the audience members sign their name on the slit card on both sides, between the double slits. This way, they can see that you have not switched cards.

TWENTY-ONE
CARD TRICK

EFFECT

Find a card in an impossible way.

ROUTINE

Ask a friend to shuffle a deck of cards. Then have him count off twenty-one cards onto a separate pile and place the remaining cards aside.

Take the twenty-one cards and lay them out, face up, in three columns of seven cards.

Ask your friend to mentally select a card and tell you which column it's in.

Scoop up the three columns of cards and lay them out again. Ask your friend to tell you again which column his card is in.

For the last time, lay out the columns in the same way and ask your friend to tell you which one contains his card.

At this point, scoop up that one column and hold the cards so that only you can see the faces.

Take one card and lay it facedown on the table.

Ask your friend to name the card he selected.

Turn over the card you laid on the table and show it to be your friend's card.

PROPS

a deck of cards

METHOD

Step 1

Lay out the cards in the following way:

```
A  B  C
X  X  X
X  X  X
X  X  X
X  X  X
X  X  X
X  X  X
X  X  X
```

First card in column A, next in B, next in C; then start again; next in A, next in B, and so on, until all twenty-one cards are laid out. The top card should be overlapped by the next.

Step 2

After your assistant mentally selects a card and tells you which column it's in, scoop up one of the other columns into a pile and leave it on the table, face up. Scoop up the indicated column and place it on

Laying out the cards

top of the first pile. Now scoop up the third column and place it on the accumulated pile.

Pick up the pile you've just assembled and turn it over, so that it's facedown. Deal off the cards one at a time, turning them faceup. Lay them out in the order of step 1. Once again, start with column A, then B, then C.

Repeat the process, beginning with column A. Continue until all of the cards are dealt.

When you have completed this, there should be three columns of seven cards each, the top card overlapped by the next. Ask your friend to indicate again the column with the selected card.

Step 3

For the last time, scoop up the cards as in step 2, leaving the pile from the selected column between the two other piles, and lay them out again in three columns of seven cards each.

Step 4

After your friend once again indicates the selected column, look at the fourth card from the top in that column. That is the selected card.

NOTE

When the cards are laid out in this way, they form a mathematical matrix. Once again, math has helped us to create a great trick.

MATCH GAME

EFFECT

Once you know the secret, you'll never lose this game.

ROUTINE

Two players, taking from twenty matchsticks, pick up one, two, or three matches on each turn. Whoever picks up the last remaining match is the loser.

PROPS

20 matchsticks (or 20 coins, slips of paper, pieces of candy, etc.)

METHOD

No matter who goes first, you will win if you follow this basic formula:

With each draw, be sure that you leave your opponent with seventeen, thirteen, nine, or five matches. These are the key numbers. Once you leave your opponent one of these amounts, you can't lose.

When leaving a key number of matches, calculate how many to take on your next turn by looking at the remaining matches in groups of four. See how many matches your opponent takes, then take enough to make that total four.

If he takes one, you take three.

If he takes two, you take two.

If he takes three, you take one.

This puts you automatically at the next key number.

If you have to select against a key number (17, 13, 9, or 5), take only one match, giving yourself the greatest opportunity to hit a key number.

If you start the game, take three matches on your first move.

NOTE

Mathematicians call this *The Game of Nim.* It has been described as "a mathematically perfect game."

To win the game every time, you must use a "system." Once you have the system working for you (hitting a key number), you can't lose, unless you make a mistake in subtracting groups of four.

BETCHA'S

EFFECT

Betcha's are quick games that are almost impossible for you to lose.

ROUTINE

Phone Book Proposition 1

Say to a friend, "Betcha that if you open up a phone book to any page and mark off twenty successive numbers (numbers in a row), out of those twenty numbers there will be at least two phone numbers that have the same last two digits (for example, 4216 and 8316)."

At first glance, it appears that your friend has the odds in his favor. There are 100 possible combinations for those last two digits (from 00 to 99). Therefore,the odds seem to be 5 to 1 against you.

Mathematically, however, the odds are 7 to 1 in your favor.

In other words, every 100 times you play this Betcha, you will lose only thirteen times.

Phone Book Proposition 2

Your friend probably will be getting annoyed after you've played Phone Book Proposition 1 a few times. Now it's time to play a different version.

Say to your friend: "I'm going to give you a chance to win. Open the phone book and mark off the last two digits of any number. Count down forty-five numbers, and I'll betcha that those two numbers you marked off won't appear as the last two digits of any of those forty-five numbers. Don't forget, you're getting more than twice as many numbers to work with as I had just a minute ago."

This game is also heavily weighted in your favor. In the first game, you were allowed to match *any* two numbers. In this game, your friend must match a specific number. The odds are greater than 3 to 2 that he will fail.

In other words, out of every 100 times that you play this game, you will win 60 times.

Birthday Proposition

Here's a great Betcha for a group of about forty people.

Say to the group: "I betcha that there are at least two people here with the same birthday."

Most people who try to figure this out assume that, since there are 365 days in the year, the chance that two people in a group of forty will have the same birthday is about 1 in 10 (out of every 100 tries, there will be only 10 successes). However, your real chance of success is about 8 to 1. Out of every 100 tries, you will be correct about 87 times.

Here's the math behind this trick. When the second person is asked for his birthday, chances that it is not the same as the first person's are 364/365. Multiply that by 363/365 for the third person,

362/365 for the fourth, etc. The numerator decreases by one each time. The odds are 50 to 50 or 1 to 1 between the twenty-second and twenty-third person. By the time you reach the fortieth person, the odds are 8 to 1 in your favor.

NOTE

These Betcha's seem to be fair propositions, but actually they are heavily weighted in your favor, according to the theory of probability. This theory, first developed by Blaise Pascal in the seventeenth century, explains the chances that something will occur. In a situation (such as the chances of two of forty people sharing a birthday), each possible outcome is assigned a number, called a probability measure, that represents its chances of occurring.

chemistry

In the following section, many of the tricks involve chemicals that are dangerous to use, or can be dangerous if handled improperly. Use extreme caution when working with these chemicals. Do not get any of them in your eyes or mouth or on your clothing. Be sure that an adult assists you when you practice these particular tricks. *Caution* is the name of the game here.

GHOST IN
THE GLASS

Before you attempt to perform this trick, have an adult (a teacher or parent) read the instructions and help you practice in a safe manner.

EFFECT

A ghost materializes in a sealed glass.

ROUTINE

Say the following to your audience:

"Most people think that ghosts don't exist, but I can tell you from personal experience that those people are wrong.

"I have found a way to actually prove that specters come to visit us on this mortal plane. I've put together a ghost chamber for the purpose of capturing a spirit for a short time."

Display a drinking glass and a plain glass ashtray, and say the following:

"Of course, as everyone knows, ghosts rarely make their presence known in daylight. Instead of darkening the room, we're going to cover the ghost chamber with a handkerchief."

At this point, you may go into a "trance" or just ask the spirits to make their presence known.

Whatever method you choose to conjure up the spirits, remove the handkerchief from the glass after a few moments. A smoky form can be seen inside.

"Here is the proof that I've told you about. Now it is time for the spirit to depart."

Remove the ashtray from the mouth of the glass, tip the glass on its side, and say, "And now the ghost dissipates, returning from whence it came."

PROPS

a drinking glass or brandy snifter
a glass ashtray or glass plate, large enough to rest
    on top of the drinking glass or snifter but not
    so large as to be awkward
a handkerchief or bandanna

THE NEXT ITEMS MUST BE HANDLED WITH CAUTION! To be safe, it would be best if you got some small amounts of the following from a chemistry teacher:

hydrochloric acid or muriatic acid
ammonium hydroxide (laboratory-grade ammonia)

All of these chemicals are dangerous. Keep them away from your skin and eyes. Do not spill any on your clothes. These chemicals should be in stoppered bottles. Each should have its own eyedropper or pipette for measuring.

METHOD

Before your performance, put a small amount (five to seven drops) of ammonia into the drinking glass or snifter. Carefully swirl it around so that the inside of the glass has a light coating. Put the glass aside.

Put two or three drops of acid in the ashtray or dish. Keep the glass and the ashtray away from each other so that the chemical reaction does not take place at the wrong time, ruining the trick.

While reciting your patter, place the ashtray, acid side down, over the mouth of the glass and quickly cover the glass and ashtray with the handkerchief.

The trick now works by itself.

NOTE

When ammonia, a base, mixes with an acid, insoluble salts are formed. The salts are very fine and lightweight, and can stay suspended in air for a short while. They give the appearance of smoke, or in this case, the illusion of a ghost.

MYSTIC SANDS

EFFECT

Different colored sands are dropped into a bowl of water and stirred. As if by magic, they are removed dry and separated by color.

ROUTINE

Say the following to your audience: "Here are three piles of sand, each a different color, coming from the different deserts of the world."

Reach into each pile and show the sand to be free flowing.

"You see before me a bowl of water representing the oceans of the world. Long, long ago, the oceans were in turmoil."

With this, stir the water with one hand. The water turns dark.

"The sands of the world were thrown about by the wild winds, eventually landing in the oceans."

Take a handful of sand from each pile. Place the sand into the bowl of water.

"The winds whipped the oceans into a fury, mixing the sands together."

Once again, use your hand to stir the water.

"A great magician was called upon by the leaders of the world to bring the beautiful sands back to their homelands. Using magic, he was able to reach into the oceans and extract the sand, color by color, drying them out at the same time, returning them to their rightful places on earth."

Reach in and take out the sand, color by color.

"He then waved his hand through the oceans, calming them to a peaceful state."

Brush your hand through the water. It turns clear, with no sand to be seen.

PROPS

3 different colored sands—red, green, and blue—
   available from an aquarium supply store in 2-
   pound packages
3 ounces paraffin wax
old pots and pans
decorative bowls
a large, clear, glass bowl filled with water
coffee filter paper

Take one color of sand and place it in a pot. Add a 1-ounce piece of paraffin.

Place this pot into a larger pot containing boiling water. Slowly heat the sand mixture. *Be careful.* If paraffin is overheated, it can catch on fire. Have an adult supervise this.

Stir the sand mixture well, making sure that all of the sand is lightly coated with wax. Add more wax if necessary.

Set the pot aside to cool and harden.

Do the same with the other two batches of sand.

When each sand mixture has cooled, take it out of its pot and break it up until you have what appears to be free-flowing sand. You can grind it by rubbing it through a strainer. Place each batch in an individual decorative bowl.

THE FOLLOWING CHEMICALS ARE NECESSARY FOR THIS TRICK, BUT SHOULD BE TREATED WITH RESPECT. THEY CAN BE DANGEROUS.

ferric ammonium sulfate (powder)
tannic acid powder
oxalic acid powder

Dissolve the ferric ammonium sulfate (⅛ teaspoon) in the bowl of water.

Place ⅛ teaspoon of tannic acid into the center of a 3-inch square of coffee filter paper or paper towel and tightly twist it into a pouch.

Place ¼ teaspoon of oxalic acid into the center of a 3-inch square of coffee filter paper or paper towel and tightly twist it into a pouch.

METHOD

Follow the actions outlined in the *Routine* section.

When first stirring the water (". . . the oceans were in turmoil"), secretly pick up the tannic acid packet and swish it through the water in the clear glass bowl. The tannic acid reacts with the ferric ammonium sulfate, causing the water to turn black.

Next, sift the first batch of colored sand. As you are about to put the sand in the water, squeeze it with two hands. The sand will stick together because of the paraffin. Gently lay the ball of sand on the bottom of the bowl. Do this with each batch of sand.

As you stir the water a second time ("The winds whipped the ocean into a fury . . ."), make sure that you do not hit the sand balls in the bottom of the bowl.

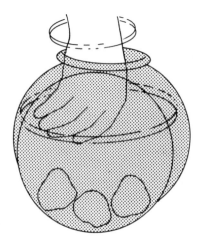

When this is done, it appears to the audience as though the sands are well mixed.

Reach into the bowl and take out the clumps of sand, one by one. As you bring them over to their individual bowls, crush them and the sand will flow freely between your fingers.

After the last ball of sand is retrieved, secretly pick up the packet with oxalic acid and swish your hand through the bowl of water. The acid causes the water to become clear.

BE SURE TO WASH YOUR HANDS WELL AFTER PERFORMING THIS TRICK.

NOTE

The sand appears to stay dry because it is coated with wax. It sticks together because the wax has an adhesive quality. The water changes color due to reactions between the different chemicals.

SIGNED
IN BLOOD

EFFECT

Magically slice your arm with a knife and use your blood to sign a contract.

ROUTINE

Tell the following story to your audience:

"There are stories about people who made pacts with the devil. These people sold their souls and in return were given whatever they wished on earth. One of the more famous stories is 'The Devil and Daniel Webster.'

"Part of the story usually includes the signing of the satanic contract with the blood of the soul-selling mortal. I'd like to show you what that might look like. Be aware that this is just a trick, and that there is nothing on earth that would make me sell my soul.

"I'll write a short contract now."

Write out the following with a blue ballpoint pen:

I [write your name] *will never sell my soul to the devil.*

When that's done, take out a knife, sterilize it in a jar of antiseptic, then run it across your arm. It looks as though you've actually sliced through the flesh when a nasty streak of "blood" appears on your arm.

Pick up the blue ballpoint pen, dip it into the blood, and sign your name to the contract.

PROPS

a blunt knife
a solution of ferric chloride (1 quart)
a solution of sodium thiocyanate (1 quart)
a jar labeled *"antiseptic"*
a Chromatic® brand pen. This pen has two cartridges, one red, one blue, which are easily switched.
a piece of paper

Do not attempt this trick if you have a cut or scrape on your arm. Chemicals can be dangerous if handled improperly.

METHOD

Prior to performing this trick, paint your arm, where you want the cut to appear, with ferric chloride. Let it dry. Do not perform this trick if you have any broken skin.

The Performance:
Write the contract, as described in the *Routine* section.

Roll up your sleeve to the part of your arm that's coated with ferric chloride.

Next, "sterilize" the knife in the jar of "antiseptic," really the sodium thiocyanate. Let the knife remain wet.

Carefully make a cutting motion across your arm with the knife. A "bloodstain" will appear.

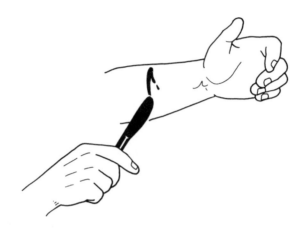

Pick up the pen that you have used to write the contract, switch the cartridges when you pick it up, dip it into the "blood" on your arm, and sign the contract in blood.

When the trick is concluded, thoroughly wash your arms and hands.

NOTE

A blood-red color results when ferric chloride and sodium thiocyanate come in contact with each other.

BLOODY FINGERPRINT

EFFECT

A magical detective (you) has been called in to find the perpetrator of a crime. The guilty person is found by "the Bloody Fingerprint detector."

ROUTINE

In your best Sherlock Holmes impression, say:

"I've asked everyone here today to help me solve the theft of the famous Werther jewels. We've known for some time that one of you was the brains behind this crime. Tonight we will find out who that person is.

"I have six identical envelopes here, each holding a folded index card. One index card is marked with an X. The person holding it is the criminal."

Show the sealed envelopes, shuffle them, and pass them out to six people. No one knows the criminal's identity.

"Now, all that you have to do is touch your finger into this lie detector fluid, then touch that finger to your envelope. The outcome is certain."(The lie detector fluid is actually a bowl of water.)

When the participants have all done this, one envelope stands out from the rest. That envelope is imprinted with a bloody fingerprint.

The participants open their envelopes and find the index cards blank, except for the x on the card from the envelope with "the bloody fingerprint."

PROPS

a bowl of water, containing 2 to 4 ounces of household ammonia
6 identical envelopes
6 index cards, one marked with an X
a solution of phenolphthalein mixed with alcohol

Coat the outside of one envelope with the above solution, allowing it to dry before you continue.

Fold the index cards in half.

Insert one card into each envelope. Put the card marked with an X into the treated envelope.

Seal the envelopes.

Do this before the performance.

METHOD

Follow the routine outlined above. The trick pretty much works by itself. You will have to experiment with the amount of ammonia to be used. Use the smallest amount possible so that the odor permeates the area as little as possible. And, again, remember to be careful when handling these liquids.

NOTE

Phenolphthalein is used to indicate if a compound is a base. In the presence of a base, it turns bright red.

physiology

HEARTBEAT OF A FAKIR

EFFECT

You stop your heartbeat.

ROUTINE

Tell your audience a story about Hindu fakirs, traveling street magicians from India, and some of the wonders that they have accomplished: lying on a bed of nails, charming snakes, and performing the famous East Indian Rope Trick.

Go on to tell them the following:

"A fakir would throw one end of a rope high in the air, where it would remain suspended. A young Jadwallah boy would climb to the top of the rope and vanish in a puff of smoke.

"And now for the Famous East Indian Rope Trick. But first, we need a young Jadwallah boy."

Wait a moment, then say: "No Jadwallah boy! No East Indian Rope Trick!"

When the laughter has subsided, tell the audience:

"Fakirs could actually control their pulses, slowing down their hearts until they stopped, restarting them at their own will. They could put their bodies into suspended animation. I'll demonstrate that for you now."

At this point, have a helper from the audience come up and find the pulse point in your left wrist.

When it's found, tell him to notice how the pulse is slowly becoming weaker until it totally stops. At this point he should tell the audience that there is no pulse.

Apparently, you have stopped your heart.

Your helper will feel the pulse return, until once again it is normal.

PROPS

a small ball, like a golf ball or handball

METHOD

Conceal the ball under your left armpit. By pressing your left arm tightly against your body, the artery running down your arm will be partially blocked. *If you do this for only a few moments at a time, no damage will occur.*

When the artery is blocked, the pulse stops, making it seem as though you have stopped your heart.

To restart the pulse, all you have to do is relax your arm and take the pressure off the artery.

NOTE

The pulse that is felt in your wrist is an indicator of how many times a minute your heart is beating.

The ancillary artery runs down your arm from the heart. The beats are felt at your wrist, where the artery runs close to the skin.

To find your pulse, have your helper place his middle and index fingers on the inside of your wrist. Stand quietly. In a few moments, he should notice the slight pulsing caused by blood flowing through the artery. Once he feels it, slowly apply pressure to the ball. Your helper will feel the pulse getting weaker, finally stopping. *To be on the safe side, do not stop the pulse for more than ten seconds at a time.*

HUMAN BRIDGE

EFFECT

Have someone's body grow rigid enough to support another person's weight.

ROUTINE

Say the following to your audience:

"I've been practicing the science of hypnosis and have been successful in placing some subjects into a deep trance. I need the help of two people from the audience."

Select two helpers.

Have one person, your hypnotic subject, stand erect, facing you. Your other helper should stand behind the subject and get ready to catch him by the shoulders when hypnosis sets in.

In a melodramatic way, say the following to your subject:

"You are growing tired, your body is getting stiffer. Your body grows rigid as you get tired. Sleep!"

With that, your subject nods off and slowly starts to fall backward.

The other helper grabs him by the shoulders. You grab the subject by the ankles and place him outstretched between two folding or kitchen chairs—his shoulders on one chair, his ankles on the other.

"The subject is now under my total control."

Once the subject is lying down, have the other assistant help balance you for the next part.

Take off your shoes and slowly stand on the subject's body, one foot on his chest, one foot on his thighs.

"Our subject is as solid as a bridge."

Step down.

PROPS

3 chairs
2 assistants

METHOD

This is not hypnosis. We use that patter, or story, as a reason for doing this trick. Hypnosis does work, but it is beyond the scope of this book.

The "hypnotic" subject should be a friend who has practiced this trick with you before.

In your best impression of a movie hypnotist, move your hands in front of his face.

Have him keep his body as rigid as possible, his arms stiffly held at his side.

One thing that might help is for him to extend his arms as far down his legs as he can, keeping them rigid, and grab a small bit of pants leg in each hand. Then, he should slightly arch his back a little.

Arch back. Grab a small bit of pants leg.

The human bridge

When your helper is lying between the two chairs, use the third chair as a stepladder.

Do not step on his solar plexus, or midsection, or other tender areas.

Gently step onto his chest. Do not jump. You could also sit on either side of his midsection.

If your friend is not frail, two people can sit on either side of his midsection. This is a truly impressive mock-hypnosis stunt.

Once you have "proven" that you have hypnotized the subject, have your assistant help place him upright and then "awaken" him from his trance. A hypnotist would say, "When I count backwards from five to one, you will slowly awaken, becoming fully awake when I reach one. You will remember nothing that has happened.

"Five, four, three, you're becoming wide awake, two, one. Wake up!"

NOTE

The body is a powerful instrument, and the physical structure of the bones and muscles permits this effect. Just remember that if you put all of your weight on your subject's midsection, he would fold up like a book and would be unable to support you.

A diver uses these same muscles to help hold his body rigid as he enters the water. A dancer uses the same technique for certain routines.

CONCLUSION

Now you have a whole arsenal of magic tricks to fool your friends. These tricks may be performed one at a time or strung together to produce a complete magic show. Practice these tricks, and I'm sure that you'll fool everyone who sees them.

I hope that you've enjoyed reading this book and learning some of its secrets. In addition to learning about magic, I hope that you've also discovered that science can be interesting and fun.

FOR FURTHER READING

Gardner, Robert. *Science Experiments*. New York: Franklin Watts, 1988.

Goldwyn, Martin. *How a Fly Walks Upside Down*. New York: Citadel Press, 1979.

Macaulay, David. *The Ways Things Work*. Boston: Houghton-Mifflin, 1988.

White, Laurence B., Jr., and Ray Broekel. *Optical Illusions*. New York: Franklin Watts, 1986.

SUPPLIERS

EMUND SCIENTIFIC CO.
101 E. Gloucester Pike
Barrington, NJ 08007-1380

Send for their free catalog.
It's filled with all sorts
of scientific apparatus.

FREY SCIENTIFIC
905 Hickory Lane
Mansfield, OH 44905

Ask your teacher to send for this
free science catalog. The request
must be on school stationery.

LOUIS TANNEN, INC.
6 West 32nd St.
New York, NY 10001-3808

Great magic store. Greatest magic
catalog. Catalog costs $8.50 plus
$2.50 postage. Mention you read
about them in Friedhoffer's book.

PAUL DIAMOND'S MAIL ORDER MAGIC
P.O. Box 11570
Fort Lauderdale, FL 33339

Good prices. Tell Paul that you
want his free price list as seen
in Friedhoffer's book.

ABRACADABRA MAGIC SHOP
Department C-448
P.O. Box 463
Scotch Plains, NJ 07076

$2.00 gets you a catalog and
a six-month subscription to
the monthly newsletter.

HANK LEE'S MAGIC FACTORY
125 Lincoln Street
Boston, MA 02205

Great magic store. Good catalog!
Inquire as to cost.
Mention Friedhoffer.

ABBOTT'S MAGIC CO.
Colon, MI 49040

Good catalog! Inquire as to cost.

INDEX

ABOUT
THE AUTHOR

Friedhoffer has studied magic for
many years, ultimately receiving a
"Doctor of Arcane Letters" degree
from Miskatonic University in
Arkham, Massachusetts. He performs
all over the United States at such
places as the White House, colleges
and universities, trade shows, nightclubs,
society functions, and television shows.
He lives in New York City.